IMPERFECT LODGINGS

Poems

Pete Mesling

Other Kingdoms Publishing, Seattle

PUBLICATION HISTORY

The most important thing about dreams is the existence in them of magical emotions, to which waking Consciousness is not ordinarily sentient. Awe of vast constructions; familiar eternal halls of buildings; sexual intensity in rapport; deathly music; grief awakenings, perfected lodgings.

ALLEN GINSBERG,
JOURNALS: EARLY FIFTIES, EARLY SIXTIES

Therefore God becomes as we are, that we may become as he is.

WILLIAM BLAKE,
THERE IS NO NATURAL RELIGION

CONTENTS

THE PRIMAL SYMPATHY

I miss a thing that never was.
I miss it most, in fact, because
It never yet has let me down—
But then, it has not yet been found.

It's like a thing within a dream
Or in a painting, though it seems
That really it's what lies behind
The images that come to mind.

For instance, not the looming cloud
That serves the painting as a shroud,
That tries to keep the battered house
Protected, as it would a mouse.

And not the golden stalks that part
Before the plowman and his art.
But maybe something in the way
A window in the house was made.

A streak or two of darkest hues
Is what effects the comely ruse
That from that shadowed window pane
A face looks out in fear, in vain.

It may not even be the case
That I was meant to see a face,
Yet there it is for me to see,
Imagined or compulsory.

Or looking past the painter's brush,
I find the same unbidden hush.
In lyre and drum, in tales of yore—
In acting, dance, and others, for ...

It's not the notes upon the sheet
That fill me up with kindled heat.
It's how they're played and what's between

That tells me what they truly mean.

And when I read the truest words,
It's music like I've never heard,
A kind of song that will not wage
Its restless wars upon the page.

A sculptor, I've been told, need not
Know how to sculpt an aspect sought,
But only have the smarts to know
He's done it when the clay is so.

And if no art is near at hand
My curiosity might land
Upon the works of Nature's will:
From dale to wood to sea to hill.

Though hidden mostly in the night,
By day few things give more delight.
Just as the moon and stars by day
Are hidden but at night are gay.

I miss a thing I cannot name.
I miss it though it never came.
It speaks to me without a sound
Yet seems to make the world go round.

LIVING AND DYING

Dying is not a thing to come.
It's already here, happening all the time.
That wrinkle in the mirror since a week ago Tuesday
Is all the proof you should need of mortality.

Too bad we do not foresee our own births
So we could revel in the anticipation,
As we tremble with fear at the song of the death-bird
That sings from every shadow.

SOMEONE TO BLAME

I'd rather be dead than dying,
But I'd rather be dying than dead.
The paradox between the two
Is doing in my head.

So instead of playing mind games,
I'll take it out on you.
I'd rather be dead than dying,
But not all of our dreams come true.

WITHOUT MERCY, WITHOUT WRATH

Is there no god in this heavenly hell?
No devil to queer the stagnant hum?
No threat of hurled vituperation?
No hesitation when sin comes calling?
No longing hauled from the long haul of living?
No trying, though dying, to push back the night?

No crying for strangers with histories of shadow?
No public displays of unalloyed disgust?
No wandering the streets without purpose or cause?
No questioning nerve unconcerned with approval?
No justice for fools or their jubilant mobs?
No god and no devil to save us from ourselves?

THE CONTENTED FARMER

I have never slept so soundly
As I slept to the crepitation
Of my corn
On fire
In the night:
A chorus of cremation,
A peripheral flicker of endings,
A sharp odor of avoidable waste,
A soft breeze of freedom through an open window …

All of my days since have been filled with want and anxiety,
But that one night was a fine, pure, truthful bliss.

FREE AT LAST

Facing the tide she knows so well,
Hearing it more than seeing it in this late blue hour,
Drawing the mist of salt air into her nostrils,
She watches the bright moon shatter across the waves.

Learning to *go* free in the world
Is so different from *being* free, she muses.
Easy for some, difficult for others.
She has not yet developed a knack for it.

It is no suicide gravity that holds her near the water
But a curiosity about what comes before life, and after.
If the sea cannot speak of such things,
What hope does she have of learning them in this world?

She backs away, then steps forward again,
Even closer to the lapping surf than before.
Part of her believes she could swim across the ocean if she tried.
Part of her knows this to be an impossible fantasy.

As unconvinced of the world as ever,
She stoops down to wash his drying blood from her hands,
Then turns her back on the truth of the waters
And climbs the sandy beach to her car.

SUNSET

A hesitant shoal of pink offers the mountains illusory protection from the coming dark of night:
One last act of beauty for the day.

RAISON D'ETRE

Naked and bald, Death rides in on his oversized goat.
Together they clamber up cliffs and ravage villages.
They roil oceans in their wake
And collapse caves with their subterranean prancing,
All in service of misery.

What good is any of it?

Better to ask the fiddler why he bows,
Or the preacher why he tames his flock,
Or the merchant why he earns beyond his needs.
There can be only one truthful answer:
It is the sport of the thing that matters.

CAPTURED IN A FALL

Our frailty is perfectly captured in a fall.
The toe of our shoe catches a slab of sidewalk,
Canted by no more than half an inch
(More we would have noticed).

The loss of balance is shocking.
Disbelief follows us to the ground,
Where we crumple,
Embarrassed more than pained.

"Why have I been hurt?"
We wonder.
"Why has this happened to me?"
But it has.

Our frailty is perfectly captured in a fall,
Whether the audience is one or all.

THE FREEDOM OF THE GULL

Fighting the winter wind fills the gull with joy,
A show supported by a memory of abundance.
She trusts that her next meal will come,
But there are no guarantees in the leaflessness of winter,
And she will be hungry from her sky dance.

Maybe true happiness only comes when we give up caring
For our needs and comforts,
If only for a short time,
Choosing instead to pursue the thrill of the wing.

Not all is hunting.
Not all is play.
And the balance between them is uneven.
Still, the one gives meaning to the other.

And so the gull flies,
That man may dream.

She harbors no jealousy of our brooding existence,
Us prisoners of gravity.

And so the gull perishes,
Without having seen it coming.

NIGHT DRIVE

Corn stalks flutter as if alive at the fringe of my headlights.
The wind bends them, but not all in the same direction.
Maybe *it* is sentient, too:
Serpentine,
Invisible,
Strong,
Until it burns itself out.

Or does a pair of imps flank the two-lane road,
Racing through the corn at highway speed,
Waiting for the perfect opportunity to bolt in front of my car
And scare me into a fatal accident,
Themselves impervious,
As they seek out a thrill kill?
I can almost hear their trickling laughter.

I cover the brake with my foot,
But the cornfields end like city blocks.

CROSSING THE RIVER: A HAIKU

Crossing the river
Was easy when he was young.
Now he stays ashore.

THE POSSIBILITIES

If a peace that spread and a hand that stayed and a mouth that silenced doubt ...
If an angel fell into deepest hell and a lucky soul ran out ...

If a mocking laugh, if a warning growl, if a sword put down unused ...
If a truth revealed, if a fear concealed, if a talent that's misused...

If a troubled man, if a hopeless friend, if a sickly, dying beast ...
If a cross ignored, if a god implored, if the wingless demons feast ...

If the face turns down, if the heart beats low, if compassion fades away ...
If the tree, not heard by a distant bird, takes its chances anyway ...

If a light switched off is remembered best for the things it did not show ...
If the world relied on the things untried and the facts it does not know ...

If the darkness were an imagined woe and the scales of justice true ...
If the masses could only hope to learn what I hope to learn from you ...

AN ECHO ACROSS TIME

The tolling of a medieval bell
Still rolls like a wind across deserts and plains.
This bell was struck in honor of the dead,
Its ringer also dead now.

CONTRARY WINDS: A PARADELLE

Can you bear the burden of your sorrow?
Can you bear the burden of your sorrow?
How long will it last tonight?
How long will it last tonight?
Of the last burden, your long sorrow can bear
How you will it tonight!

I rest by the water and wait for daylight.
I rest by the water and wait for daylight.
You are alive, there in the darkness somewhere.
You are alive, there in the darkness somewhere.
Darkness by the water; rest there and wait.
For somewhere you are I, out in the daylight.

And fresh life will creep into the heart;
And fresh life will creep into the heart.
Old skin is shed at the end of this winter.
Old skin is shed at the end of this winter.
Creep into this shed of old skin!
Is life, at the heart, fresh, and will the winter end?

Into the sorrow you creep:
The heart is of long, fresh darkness.
How will this old life bear the winter and wait there for daylight?
I shed you in the end.
Tonight—somewhere—it can rest at last, your burden.
Water and skin are of ... alive by ... the will.

VARIABLE DESTINIES

He lost his sense of gratitude on a lonely walk through misty woods.
Beauty all around him, he fell into despair.
Where were you then?
Where were any of us?
All he needed was something to return to,
Some scrap of belief in himself.
But the ancient, towering firs stood rooted in indifference
And the damp air gave no quarter.
So he walked on, slick fir needles sticking to his boots,
Until at last the forest broke and he stood at the edge of a cliff.
We're told these things come down to a matter of choice.
He wasn't so sure.
If he could have chosen to throw himself into that void,
Surely he would have, and avoided more days of restless contemplation.
But there he stood, as incapable of taking a final leap
As he would have been to smother a child.
To him these things were not options to be chosen or dismissed.
Either they were in the blood or they were not.
They were *not* in his blood, but blood is mutable.
Maybe his has thickened against life since that day,
But I doubt he could find that cliff again if he wanted to.

A RETURN TO CHAOS

Acres of sludge gurgle up out of the sea, boiling hot and viscous.
Mountains topple and shift,
Their broken summits stabbing at swirling clouds of indigo,
Like giant, ineffectual spearheads.

Oceans churn in all directions,
Already having claimed the cities.

Now there is no end result to predict, or hope for, or avoid—
No one left to do the predicting, hoping, or avoiding.
There is only the idiot grin of myriad stillborn futures,
And the present, with its trapped histories breaking free like poison spores.

DECEIVED

The adult he dreamed of becoming
Was based on the view from his youth.
The adult he in fact became
Was the result of breaching the unknown.

POOR BUSTER KEATON'S BOAT

Poor Buster Keaton's boat.
The day of sailing before him is a perfect fantasy,
Spoiled only when he launches the vessel from shore
And watches it follow the lake bottom's incline to a watery grave.

Buster's face tells us the boat was his central self,
An unsteerable soul in search of predictability,
But given only shock after shock after shock,
Until it had no more to give in return.

Poor Buster Keaton's boat.
Perhaps it is the central self of us all.
Who is at the helm here, if anyone?
To what time is this thing tethered, and to what place?

Poor Buster Keaton,
The way he hauls his boat so diligently into the water,
Only to have it refuse to float.
Poor all of us and our hopeful boats.

DREAMCATCHER

I thought I had lost another dream
To the lethargic gauze of sunlight
That crept into my room that morning
And bound me to the bed.

By the time I gave in to the day's pulse,
The lost dream was Poe's watch enveloped in cotton:
An inscrutable guilt.

I found my dream again at last and hooked it
From the dark swirls of my morning coffee.

Now I long for it to come true.

A DARK AGE

We transplant hearts.
We send rovers to Mars.
We fly across the globe.
We study the depths of our oceans.
We split the atom.
We educate the dull.
And still the twin mysteries of living and dying elude us.

We murder our children.
We devalue life.
We elect clowns to rodeo posts.
We fuel the creep of destitution.
We change the climate, creating unnatural disasters.
We shelve our books, preferring Twitter.
But still there are the twin mysteries of living and dying.

Still there are the twin mysteries of living and dying,
Which elude and enlighten us all.

THE BIG DARK: A MEDITATION

Grief, like a cloud,
Obscures everything except that for which we grieve—
But allows us the comfort of memories.
Depression is a heavier cloud,
A threatening darkness that descends to overwhelm,
Turning even our fondest recollections against us.

Depression is longing without hope.
Joylessly feeling joy.
Coveting but not attempting.
Having your free will revoked as punishment for an unnamed crime.

In a mildly depressive state, everything could be better:
The summer breeze on your face,
The kiss on your cheek,
The compliment paid,
The balance of your bank account,
The food on your plate,
The music you're listening to,
The world in which you live.
In the grip of severe depression, none of it's worth a damn.

Everything is the depressive's fault.
He is likely to hear all utterances as a choir of condemnation,
And he will eventually add his voice to the choir himself.

Maybe the best way out is to bore through
(Think tunnel),
Not climb out
(Think pit)
Or over
(Think mountain).
Let it change you; trust the growing light to be your guide.

Depression heeds no advice.
The only immediate reprieve comes from believing it is temporary,
Which is difficult in the moment—
And, for some, a falsehood.

No matter how profound or long lasting a bout of depression,
Someone is enduring one more profound and longer lasting.
Your next one may be better, or it may be worse, but there *will be* a next one.
These are disappointing truths.

When all artifice peels away,
Revealing a drab world overrun with human animals
Whose customs and interactions are low and predictable ...
That is depression talking.

Yet depression has an unfortunate, undeniable allure,
Providing respite from the noise and responsibilities of life.
Because of this, we invite it in—
Those of us who are prone—
As we might a vampire.

Dreams are the opposite of depression:
Freeing where depression constricts,
Compelling where depression is dull,
Alive with possibility where depression is rote in the extreme.
But dreams and depressive episodes have this much in common:
It is a relief to leave the bad ones behind.

Depression can come on like a sudden sadness,
But that only masks the sense of worthlessness that lies in wait.

At its best, depression comes with a layer of fear,
Which can keep you tethered to reality and prevent the onset of absolute apathy.

A dubious oracle,
Depression seduces us,
Reduces us to a single eye that sees only the truth.
Nothing is prettified or made polite.
That doesn't mean you're *actually* seeing the truth when you're depressed—
Only that it feels that way,
Like being drunk.

Depression is different at different ages, too.
In my twenties I could drink it away.
In my thirties I could fool myself into thinking that time was still on my side.
At midlife there is no assuaging the Dragon.
It must swallow the elderly whole.

To grow depressed is to grow self-centered in the extreme,
Which can lead to guilt and despair so heavy they're like slabs of stone
Piled onto your chest.

That horrible nagging sense that you've forgotten to do something,
But you can't quite remember what it is ...
Imagine that what you finally remember
Is having forgotten to pick up your child from school,
And now you're on a plane hundreds of miles away and your spouse is overseas.
That's anxiety.
Learning that the plane you're on will never land ...
That's depression.

As with flame, depression has no single color.

The ochres of its awakenings are oddly beautiful,
As is the surge of violet in its retreats.
But the battling reds and yellows of its burning
Are breathtaking mostly in their ferocity.

It's impossible to know for sure whether a familiar transaction with the world
Might trigger or intensify a depressive spiral,
But certain situations make me more nervous than others:
Waking from a really fine dream, for instance,
And being able to recall every glorious detail.

Depression can be a fat black crow
Flying toward you from some sudden, distant point,
Its course an erratic multitude of miscues and false starts.
That it finds you in the end is a kind of dark miracle,
For the crow is an easily distracted bird,
And none too eager for human companionship.

It is possible to be so depressed that you cannot bear to look at yourself in the mirror.
You might avert your eyes while washing your hands,
Or when stepping out of the shower.
Pity anyone whose despair regularly plummets to such a depth.

Depression is like the schoolyard bully who never fails to show his face
When you're basking in the first rays of hopeful delight you've known in weeks.
Through his taunts and insults he aims to convince you
That your joy is based on false evidence,
That you deserve to be miserable, not happy.
Never happy.
His pleasure seems to increase as yours diminishes;
He drains you of resolve and good feeling,
Leaving you ashamed of having asked for more than was your share to begin with.
You won't make the same mistake again soon.

Depression is sometimes a hell born of sound realizations,
While other times it arrives as if on a foreign wind.
This unpredictability is a loyal reminder that the demon is only ever hiding,
Thumbing its nose at any banishment you have hoped to sentence it to.

Any dent we can make in our depression, though,
Has the potential to break through the cynicism of the disease
And prove that there are steps we can take to relieve our discomfort.
If we build on those, one small step at a time,
Eventually we will emerge into daylight once more.

Depression is fatigue, illness, and a weight,
All bearing down on you at once, often suddenly.
Is it any wonder that it can be a herculean task
To pull yourself out from under all that rubble?
But if you truly wanted to give up the fight,
You would have done so long ago.
Life remains precious,

Just not as perennially enjoyable as we're led to believe.

Sometimes depression has nothing whatsoever to do with pathology
But is simply the mind and body's reaction to a psychic trauma—
As expected as being drowned in an ocean, shaken in an earthquake,
Or burned in a fire.
What is the relationship between such depression
And an underlying syndrome?
Perhaps it is like two raindrops becoming one large raindrop:
One plus one equals ONE, to paraphrase Tarkovsky.

When depression, anger, and anxiety blend together
It is like riding a raft through a maelstrom.
Getting away from it is like trying to free yourself from wood glue in a nightmare.

I feel physically heavier in the clutches of depression.
My bones press toward the earth, my skin hangs lower,
And my spirits take on mass and volume.
It is a cruel destroyer.
I cannot create, or even be productive, when deeply despondent.
A project has to matter in order for me to tackle it.
Nothing matters very much to the depressed.

When you stop being hopeful that there is hope, you are in despair.
That, too, is depression.

Depression is an ocean I call the Big Dark.
I've had seaside property on the Big Dark for a long time,
And leaving isn't an option.
I guess I'm like the guy who refuses to move off the volcano that's about to erupt.
It's my home. I'm comfortable here, and I like it fine.
But there are bad fish in those waters, and at high tide there's nowhere to run.
As a result, everything I build, I build with an acute awareness of that tide.
I've learned to be cautious when it comes to long-term planning,
To mistrust a strong sense of security or lasting tranquility.
On the other hand, I've come to appreciate the walks I take along this peculiar beach
With an intensity I wouldn't have any inkling of
If I hadn't been pulling scaly fiends out of the Big Dark since I was a boy.

Depression is a weight you carry, even when you're not fully depressed.
It's always there to remind you what might have been
If less of your time had been squandered in the Big Dark.

Yesterday was crash day.
Smooth sailing turned to rough waters as the day faded
And I failed to steer myself away from a clutch of black rocks hiding in a dark sea
At the swollen climax of twilight.
Today has been a little better, but I'm still some meters from the surface …
And running out of air.

Nothing else simultaneously fills and empties a vessel as completely as depression.
To be in its throes is to be engorged with an inky oblivion,

A nullity crammed to bulging with weightless heft,
Dimensionless mass,
And floating density.
It leaves the same way, allowing the world back in as it empties us of itself.
Some days there is little difference between being depressed and not being depressed.
Am I the yin with a black dot or the yang with a white one?
What's the difference?
C'est la vie.

Depression pleads with you to give up, yearns for your failure:
Meat, I suppose, for its endless voracity.
And oh how it wears you down!
I suspect that an overall lack of resilience marks the depressive anyway,
When compared to the normals of the world.
To have that small store diminished over time by the gnashing fangs of depression
Leaves very little room for resolve or second chances.

The Big Dark convinces us that we can measure the happiness of our lives in thimblefuls,
Even though our intellect knows it can fill canyons.

Have you ever hated yourself so much that you wished you could calve your doppelgänger
And beat it to death?
Ah, depression.

Coming out of a depression carries its own struggle,
As you start to see how easy it is to look back on your suffering as self-obsessed,
Even though you know it was not within your control to put others first while in such a state.
Then, a nagging question comes:
Is that how you seem to people, self-absorbed and limited of empathy?
Perhaps, however, the opposite is true
And it is your sensitivity and imagination that open you so wide to pain.

The worst bouts of depression seem to come during my most productive times.
I'm sailing along, thinking maybe I'm on the path to something better after all,
And *WHOOSH!*
A creature of the Big Dark rises from those brackish waters
And folds its leathery wings around me in a chilling embrace.
Then it whispers in my ear,
"Who do you think you are, rising out of mediocrity like that?
Do you honestly believe I would ever let you enjoy the kind of success you're after?
Don't make me laugh."

Is this what it's like to be a flower in bloom …
Emerging from the Big Dark into a world you don't quite remember
As being a crusher of dreams
And haven't yet discovered to be a bringer of agony?

HOLLOW THE EYE

Hollow the eye that sees no depth.
Fallow the spirit that sows discord.
Deprived the ear that hears only rage.
Wanting the hand that is used to hoard.

Rare the villain with no trace of love.
Happy the maker of things with no use.
Valued the sportsman who preys on the weak.
Doomed the betrayer and damned the noose.

Wealthy the pauper who's cast off his share.
Drowning the rich who clutch their gold.
Sullen the man who risked too little.
Buried the woman who grew too old.

Merry the young, if given the chance.
Slow to befriend, the wounded snail.
Narrow the vision that seeks to ignore.
Cruel the mechanics of Justice's scale.

SEASONAL

All of us rush to winter, then halt,
As if surprised by the sudden slowness of our surroundings.
There's much to be taken in at such a pace,
Not all of it comforting.

Eventually the engines of spring can be heard in the distance.
Though some will not make it through to the other side of winter.
Those who do bear a responsibility,
An unnamed but crucial penance.

Summer, of course, belongs to the young,
While the rest are mostly tolerated.
The play of children and lovers stakes its claim.
The wise know when to look away.

The elders get their reward in fall,
When prettiness and easy joys retreat once more,
Making room for the kind of methodical pondering
That will right the spin of the world anew.

A PERFECTLY COMPOSED PANIC

A murder of crows quickly collects on a naked tree,
And just as suddenly flutters away in a perfectly composed panic.

BLACK SKULL

A darkness came on a western wind, and an outlaw walked below.
The clouds rolled fast, and the wind smelled sharp, but the lone man's gait was slow.

In a sloping ditch, with a rock for a seat and the hill against his back,
The man unwrapped his victim's skull, but he saw it had turned black.

The skull was smooth, like a polished stone, and it felt like one in his hand.
The man could not account for the change, and he did not understand.

So when the jaws began to work, it was barely a surprise,
But when that skull began to speak, there was fear in the outlaw's eyes.

"Beyond is where you're headed," said the skull he had taken for dead.
"The same as where your enemy went who lost his only head."

"Aren't you the skull of the man I killed?" the lone man wanted to know.
"Or is this some other kind of trick to strike a similar blow?"

"My only answer isn't one you'll likely wish to hear:
I am the voice of death in life—your end is drawing near."

"Then death is not the quiet thing I've always half assumed.
But life is hard, and often cruel, and ever a path to you.

"So take me, then, to the Underworld, or wherever I'm meant to go.
I have no taste for a fight with you, or to beg you to spare my soul."

It must have been exactly what the skull had hoped he'd say,
For its words gave way to laughter, and its laughter died away.

A rent appeared in the sky above the man who'd guessed his fate,
And a lightning bolt broke free as he stood up to watch and wait.

It wasn't long before the streak of lightning found its mark.
He closed his eyes and dropped the skull and passed into the dark.

Not even a pile of ash was left to signify the hour,
And never was found the polished skull with a most unusual power.

CHIMERICAL

The mist, a symbol, softens the lake view outside my window.
Something is communicated to me in how the trees and beach houses on the far shore
Reflect in a haze onto untroubled water.

Can I hope to communicate some relevant interpretation of the impression to you?
Or can these words only serve as a limited reproduction,
A failed emulation of Nature?

The painting, the photograph, the poem …
What is added to the best of these that makes them meaningful beyond imitation?
For much is subtracted from Creation in their birth.

Yet there is an additive as well:
A spellbinding reagent that connects artist and spectator to reality—
But also to that which is beyond all known existence.

BETWEEN WARS (SELECTIONS)

Poems Inspired by Paintings from *Glitter and Doom: German Portraits from the 1920s*

Mischievous nymph in her mannish attire,
Hair pulled tight like a boy's.
Shifty match strike,
Eager to light the cigarette
That suffers between gritted teeth.
Her femininity hides within
The high-collared shirt,
Slender necktie,
Pantalooned bottom half,
And theater shoes.
But nothing hints at why
She cocks her knee so jauntily.

Deep red and voluptuous,
The dress may have been poured over her
And left traces of its hue in her magenta mop.
Who but Uriah Heep could love this crippled viper?
Who but another reddened snake
Could adore such failed mimicry of youth?
There is little her poised physique hasn't experienced,
And if we look closely enough,
We see every line of that experience
In the ghost-pale obstinacy of her face,
In the severe pencil-drawn stand-ins for eyebrows,
In the darkly outlined almonds she has instead of eyes,
The pursed sneer she has painted onto her sad lips.

"*Moi*?"
He seems to be saying
As he lays the fingers of his right hand
Against his right shoulder;
But he doesn't allow the distraction
To separate his other hand
From a flute of champagne.
His close-cropped widow's peak is half of his charm
And almost makes his satanic features okay.
The man lurking over his shoulder, however,

Has no widow's peak to hide the truth of him.

The man is a contour;
No difference between his back
And his front.
He blends into almost any background,
As long as it is florid and bent.
He wants to come across as
Unapologetically queer,
But his eyes are full of mea culpas.
The raised veins of his bald head
Hint at unredressed flares of temper,
And his claw-like fingernails
Are ready for anything.

She's seen it all from her black Victorian dress.
All the little transgressions
Her children and grandchildren
Thought escaped her notice
Were recorded with an unerring commitment
To detail.
Her arthritis made it difficult
To count her fingers,
She'd overheard Gregor say recently.
Might have been six or seven on each hand,
He'd commented.
But she knew how many fingers she had,
And a great deal more besides.
Her wisdom had not reduced her love,
But it had taken a toll on the esteem
In which she held the people of the world.

With simian apathy,
He awaits your deal-closing signature.
So much tweed for one man!
The ring on his little finger
Is shockingly red
Against the gray of his being,
A lurid touch
That must remind him
Of a past accomplishment.

He has but newly struck a bargain,
And the streaking clouds seem to know all about it,
Through the window.
His world is at an angle
And his suit hangs on him.
He must go now,

Out into the windy late afternoon.
She'll need the yellow roses
He's placed in an empty vinegar bottle
When he tells her he's lost his soul.

EXISTENCE

You're now what you were bound to be a million years ago.
A million years from now you'll be worth less than what you sow.
The nights when terror grips your throat and robs you of your sleep,
That's when the truth reveals itself to all its little sheep.
The lies we tell for comfort and the lies we think protect
Are offspring of a troubled pair: Ambition and Neglect.
So rise to serve your master once you've chosen who he'll be,
Or kneel forever at his feet and see what you can see.
And if you serve no other than yourself, I offer this:
Be careful what you ask of you; think through what you permit.

THE INNER SENSE

Art opens a sixth sense
And reminds us that not all can be known by the other five.

WHERE THE FIRE BURNS

As wind recalls the calm
And rain recalls the drought,
As fright reminds of ease
And certainty of doubt ...

As thirst belies our strength
And jokes belie ennui,
As pain gives way to mirth
And desert sand to sea ...

As beauty brings despair
And jeopardy brings hope,
As lies reveal the truth
And narrowness the scope ...

I wonder if the dark
Pertains to all I see,
And where the fire burns
When not inside of me.

CLOSE CALL

A sudden thing it was that changed my mind.
In low despondency I turned to see
A seagull startled from the underbrush.

It took my sorrow on its feathered back
And carried it away, bound for the sea,
And left me in a state of jealous awe.

SLEEP COMES NOT EASY

Distant traffic on the freeway bridge,
A thrumming ribbon of sound
Perforated by occasional outbursts
From powerful trucks,
Souped-up hotrods,
Neglected wrecks.

The approach of an airplane,
Its engine noise broken and ethereal
Until it clears the cloud cover
And steadies its guttural drone,
Revealing an intention to land.

One siren chasing through the night,
Then another—is it serious?
I never read about such things in the next day's paper,
Or of the nearby reports that may have been gunfire.

Sleep comes not easy of a summer night,
Though the windows are thrown wide
And the air is good.

Too much of life finds an open window,
Though the air is good
And the sounds are rich.

FALLOW

My crop was golden: tall and strong ...
But where are the seeds for another sowing?
Scattered thinly across the expanse of my remaining years?
Must I pick each grain as I find it,
Like a creature of the night on the scent of mustard seed?

HOPEFUL

Someday I will live
In the largest cell
There ever was.

THE ENORMOUS HOUR

Withered spruce, once strong, bending low now in the rain:
Can you recall stronger days?

If only you had vision, hearing, and voice.
But then you'd need a heart, which might get struck by an ax,
And veins, which might turn brittle in the bark.
You would also require the burden of a brain.

Maybe there's little variation to the rudiments of living and dying, though.
Perhaps it's what makes us of equal value in the end, you and me.

Even lifeless you resist falling back to the earth,
Though you must eventually.
We all must fall back to the earth
Before we can fly away forever into the enormous hour.

What are we waiting for, then?
And what is waiting for us?

THE SHADOW-BURNING SUN

The sun, burning shadows away where they hide as it arcs over the small prairie town.

Residents darting in and out of storefronts—mostly in, to escape the heat.

An old man breathing simple music through a harmonica on a bench outside Lynette's Bakery.

Secrets like tumbleweeds, blowing until they hit an obstacle that stops them in their course.

Truth dressed up in cornball humor, sputtered back and forth as acquaintances greet.

A child growing up among it all, thinking his small world is better than it turns out to be.

SLEIGHT OF HAND

My hands are easy to examine:
Tellers of tales,
In need of little coaxing.
But are they the same hands
That belonged to a twenty-year-old man?
A ten-year-old boy?
Am I the sum of my past,
Or is each new moment
Its own renewed, cell-divided life?

GRATITUDE

Thanks for the flower that pleases my eye.
Thanks for the thorn that pricks my skin.
Thanks for the rope to hang me by.
Thanks for the fire to burn it in.

Thanks for the friend who wishes me well.
Thanks for the clarion call of the dead.
Thanks for the possibility of hell.
Thanks for the heaven inside my head.

www.ingramcontent.com/pod-product-compliance
Lightning Source LLC
Chambersburg PA
CBHW020437030426
42337CB00014B/1304